ART DECO
FURNITURE AND
METALWORK

ART DECO
FURNITURE AND
METALWORK

Grange
BOOKS

A QUANTUM BOOK

Published by Grange Books
an imprint of Grange Books Plc
The Grange
Kingsnorth Industrial Estate
Hoo, nr. Rochester
Kent ME3 9ND

1-84013-113-6

This book is produced by
Quantum Books Ltd
6 Blundell Street
London N7 9BH

Project Manager: Rebecca Kingsley
Project Editor: Judith Millidge
Designer: Wayne Humphries
Editor: Clare Haworth-Maden

The material in this publication previously appeared in
*Art Deco Source Book, Art Deco: An Illustrated Guide to
the Decorative Style, Encyclopedia of Art Deco,
Art Deco: An Illustrated Guide*

QUMADFM
Set in Times
Reproduced in Singapore by United Graphic Ltd
Printed in Singapore by Star Standard Industries (Pte) Ltd

CONTENTS

INTRODUCING ART DECO

Above: a postcard advertising a Manhattan shop selling Art Deco designs.

Left: Emerson, the American firm, produced this radio in the 1930s. The red Bakelite body is typical of radios of the time.

T he term 'Art Deco' means different things to different people – but in a very specific way. To purists, for instance, it implies opulent Parisian furnishings. To students of Modernism, on the other hand, it suggests minimalism in design. To romantics the term recalls glittering Manhattan skyscrapers. And to aficionados of industrial art it evokes memories of Bakelite radios.

The school of luxuriant French design which reached its peak at the 1925 Paris World's Fair – the Exposition Internationale des Arts Décoratifs et Industriels Modernes, whence the term Art Deco is derived – is generally considered pure, high-style Art Déco (with an accent on the 'e'). Over the years, however, the output of other schools and countries of the so-called 'machine age' has come to be covered by this catch-all term, which, incidentally, was not current during the period,

and did not begin to be used until the 1960s.

Thus, the parameters of Art Deco (usually without the accent), or *Le Style 25*, as others call it, have expanded to include a wide array of modern Western architecture, design, decoration, graphics, motifs, products and even fine art dating from approximately 1915 to 1940, with the 1939–40 World's Fair in New York acting as an endpoint of sorts. Some non-French Art Deco works relate directly to Parisian design – the furniture of the German

Opposite page: William van Alen's Chrysler Building in New York is crowned by a nickel-chromed steel spire.

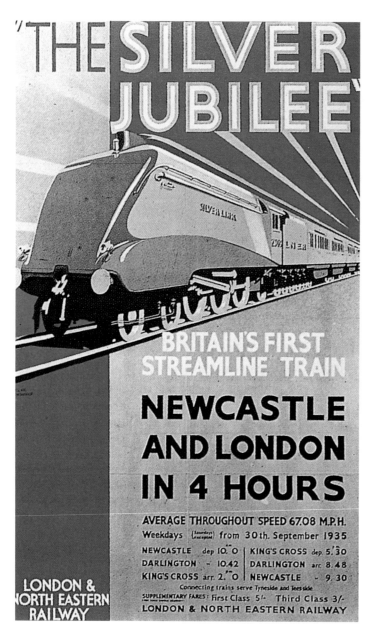

Bruno Paul or the jewellery of the American firm Black, Starr & Frost, for instance. Many other designers throughout Europe and the USA paid vestigial homage to the French style, among them the creators of the spectacular American and English motion-picture palaces, the Russian-born Serge Chermayeff, and the British potter Clarice Cliff, with her jazzy, brightly hued ceramics. Still others, such as the Bauhaus school of the Scandinavian glassmakers, created their own distinctive and original styles, blazing new and seemingly antithetical trails to those being forged by most of the French.

A MULTI-FACETED STYLE

So, far from being a school of design that is characterised only by geometric forms, or by lavishly decorated surfaces, stylised flowers, lithe female and animal figures, vivid colours and the like, as so many think of it, Art Deco is a multi-faceted style for all seasons, and for all tastes.

THE ORIGINS OF ART DECO

The seeds of Art Deco were sown well before the 1925 Paris Exposition, indeed, as early as the last years of the nineteenth and the first years of the twentieth centuries, when Art Nouveau still reigned supreme. This nature-inspired, essentially curvilinear and asymmetrical style experienced its zenith at the 1900 Exposition Universelle, which also took place in Paris, but its decline began soon afterwards, hastened in part by the rise of industrialisation. Art Deco was modern because it used aspects of machine design as inspiration. It

Left: a 1935 poster for the Silver Jubilee, *touted as 'Britain's first streamline train'. The Art Deco period was the machine age.*

was even more modern because it accelerated the adoption of such new, materials as plastic, Bakelite and chrome.

The sparks of modernism were set off in Vienna, where the architect-designers Otto Wagner (1841-1918), Josef Hoffmann (1870-1956) and Koloman Moser (1868-1918) started a trend towards rectilinearity which was to be adopted, either consciously or not, at first by French and German and later by American designers. Some of the Austrians' furniture, glass and flatware designs, even those as dating from early as 1902, are quite modern looking. In the same way, the Glaswegian Charles Rennie Mackintosh (1868-1928), who was much admired by the Viennese, created furniture, interiors and buildings which reflected an understated, proto-modern sensibility with their light colours, subtle curves and stark lines. They were a world apart from the uninhibited, undulating designs of his French contemporaries. Two Mackintosh clocks, both dating from 1917, are modern, rectilinear and architectonic. They even make use of Erinoid, a synthetic made from resin or protein plastic.

Below: a gilt and lacquered carved wood panel attributed to Paul Véra.

Right: Josef Hoffmann's masterpiece of 1905–11, the Palais Stoclet in Brussels, Belgium, demonstrates Hoffman's standing as a transitional figure between Art Nouveau and Art Deco.

Even before Mackintosh, British designers created mass-produced pieces with startling, modern looks. The silver and electroplated tableware of one of the most accomplished, Christopher Dresser (1834-1904), whose pitchers, candlesticks, tureens and tea services were designed during the 1880s ,is now displayed in such esteemed and decidedly contemporary collections as that of the Museum of Modern Art in New York.

THE ARTS AND CRAFTS MOVEMENT
The English Arts and Crafts movement, although very much grounded in medievalist principles, practices and institutions such as the guild, could also be said to have exerted some influence on

Art Deco, albeit in a surprisingly roundabout way. The lead came chiefly from its early American exponents, who then inspired later designers in the United States. Frank Lloyd Wright (1867-1959), for instance, some of whose achievements late in life were quite streamlined and Bauhaus-like, had adhered to Arts and Crafts-type aesthetic for most of his career, even when producing mass-made furniture.

EXOTIC INFLUENCES
But the French designers whose works have come to exemplify Art Deco – Emile-Jacques Ruhlmann, Jean Dunand, Armand-Albert Rateau, Süe et Mare, René Lalique *et al* – were influenced less by their immediate European

predecessors than by earlier periods, and even by far-off, exotic places, *if* they can be said to have been dependent on outside factors at all.

PRIMITIVE AND ORIENTAL ART
To trace the sources of Art Deco is indeed a difficult exercise. Since the style had so many often unrelated and even contradictory manifestations, its inspiration can only have been both manifold and diverse. Best-known among the influences are African tribal art, Central American (Aztec and Mayan) architecture and pharaonic Egyptian art, this last due in large part to the discovery of Tutankhamen's tomb in 1922. Influential as well were the bold designs and bright colours of the Ballets

Russes, the glazes and lacquerwork of the Far East and the imagery and metalwork of classical Greece and Rome. French furniture forms of the Louis XV and Louis XVI periods also contributed, and even contemporaneous fine arts such as Fauvism, Constructionism and Cubism played a part, mostly in terms of colours and shapes, especially as applied to textiles.

FUNCTIONALISM

There were, in addition, the truly modern visionaries, such as Le Corbusier (1887-1965) and his associate Charlotte Perriand (b. 1903), whose functional furniture, or 'equipment', as they termed it, was also sharply reductionist (that is, simplified to its utmost), and is still very influential today. Interestingly, Le Corbusier's stark, all-white Pavillon de l'Esprit Nouveau, at the 1925 Paris Fair, was in marked contrast to the ostentatious exhibits of Süe et Mare's Compagnie des Arts Français, Lalique,

Ruhlmann and others, yet its statement was as strongly modern – in retrospect even more so – than theirs.

INDUSTRIAL DESIGN

The exponents of the streamlined school of the Art Deco period were primarily from the United States, where industrial designers such as Raymond Loewy, Walter Dorwin Teague and Walter von Nessen helped to define modern culture with their tableware, hardware, household appliances, automobiles and aircraft. Though blatantly antithetical to the Gallic school, the work of these talented Americans shaped the future in a positive, exciting way that was not at all grounded in a romantic and ornamented past.

THE CROSS-FERTILIZATION OF STYLES

Other Americans, however, borrowed colourful, decorative elements from their French counterparts and included them in their

Above: a figure of a Japanese fan-dancer from the Preiss-Kassler workshop, c.1929. Oriental art inspired Art Deco.

Left: a macassar ebony, marquetry, giltwood and marble commode made by the Compagnie des Arts Français.

Above: this Mornington & Weston baby grand piano and stool, c.1930, incorporates architectonic elements into its design.

modern architectural creations. Structures like the Chrysler and Chanin buildings in Manhattan were latter-day temples of a kind, but devoted to industry and business rather than to any spiritual deity. Architects throughout the United States working in their own Art Deco vein created factories, apartment complexes, hotels, and, of course, film theatres. Indeed, although the Parisian architect-designers were responsible for buildings as well as for interiors and furnishings, it was their New World counterparts who really excelled in these large-scale works.

INTERDISCIPLINARY INFLUENCES

The Art Deco period is renowned for its contributions to other disciplines, as well as to architecture, furniture and industrial design. These include textiles and carpets, fashion, bookbinding, graphics (embracing posters, typography and advertising) and two entirely new fields in their time: lighting and cinema. Glass, ceramics, silver and other metalwork, jewellery, painting and sculpture were also treated in entirely Art Deco ways.

Indeed, one of the most important aspects of the 1925 Exposition was the impact of pavilions on the four major Paris department stores. Each of these stores had realised that quality and price could be supplemented by good design, and each had its own design studios. The recognition that a retail outlet could profit by employing designers provided a boost to the whole industry. Even specialist producers of glass, porcelain and ironwork at the luxury end of the market had to maintain exceptionally high standards in order to compete.

ART DECO REASSESSED

What of the Art Deco style today? The great *objets*, of course, produced at the height of

Left: a detail of William van Alen's Chrysler Building, New York City, 1930.

Below: a promotional brochure advertising the Chanin Building in Manhattan, designed by Sloan & Robertson, 1929.

the period's creativity, are prized possessions in museums and private collections, and many of the finest buildings are today being conscientiously conserved by caring enthusiasts and civic officials. Even mass-produced baubles and *bric-à-brac* are now being sought after and saved.

ART DECO'S POPULARITY TODAY

Books on the subject have proliferated since the early 1970s, covering scholarly aspects of furnishings and architecture, and making the designs of the day available to graphic artists. Dealers specialising in Art Deco – from kitsch ornaments to objects of museum quality – can be found both in big cities and country towns, and antiques fairs and auctions devoted

entirely to the period have sprung up as well. Tours of Art Deco architecture are now offered in Miami Beach, New York and Tulsa, Oklahoma, and other places will no doubt soon follow suit.

CONTEMPORARY REPRODUCTIONS

Some of the world's top designers and craftsmen are now producing furniture and architecture with Art Deco-style embellishments, and many great pieces of the 1920s have been revived by excellent contemporary reproductions. The Italian firm Cassina, for instance, offers copies of Rietveld's famous *Red and Blue Chair*. The Parisian interior designer Andrée Putman's Ecart International has brought out some of Eileen Gray's rugs and her *Transat* armchair, as well as Robert Mallet-Stevens' dining-room chairs and a Jean-Michel Frank and Chanaux sofa. Chairs by Le Corbusier, Marcel Breuer and Mies van der Rohe have become design classics which continue to be produced, and even Parker has recreated a classic 1927 fountain pen, featuring it in an advertisement along with a Cassandre poster, an Eileen Gray table and a Bauhaus lamp, all again also in production.

ART DECO REVIVED

The Cristal Lalique glass firm still makes several pieces created by René Lalique during the 1920s and 1930s, and Clarice Cliff's colourful *Bizarre* ware is being manufactured again and sold in the china departments of exclusive stores. Art Deco typefaces, graphics and colour combinations often appear in

Left: John Weinrich's pencil, paste and gouache on board perspective of New York's Rockefeller Center, c.1931 celebrates its starkly modern architecture.

Left: an elaborate wall sconce designed by the great Parisian ironworker Edgar Brandt.

Left: architect and interior designer Pierre Chareau designed this library for the 1925 Paris Exposition, where it was featured in the Ambassade Française.

Above: a collection of the highly decorated pottery of Clarice Cliff. The pieces' simple forms are jazzed up by means of daring colour combinations.

advertisements, and many stores and restaurants give prominence to Art-Deco-style fittings, furniture and menu designs. Contemporary films are frequently set in the 1920s and 1930s, with stunning period interiors and costumes, and interest in the original films themselves has intensified, with video cassettes readily available and revivals often taking place in 1930s' picture palaces.

Despite the implicit diversity of the style's theme, interest in Art Deco is not waning. The subjects and the artefacts attributed to it are likely to remain a source of fascination for decades to come. The following chapters will celebrate the Art Deco spirit as it was applied to furniture and metalwork, and will thereby show why it was that this inter-war period was among one of the richest and most exciting in design history.

FRENCH
ART DECO
FURNITURE

The period from 1905 to 1910 was a transitional one, during which the style now known as Art Deco began to evolve in Paris. Its major proponents seem to have had two primary objectives concerning design. The first was the desire to remove all traces of foreign influence in order to return to a purely French mode. As André Véra wrote: 'Thus for furniture we will . . . continue the French tradition, ensuring that the new style will be a continuation of the last international style we have, that is the Louis-Philippe style'.

Previous page: a rounded display cabinet created by Paul Follot in dark wood and ivory with a carved floral motif.

Consequently, French taste in furniture was expressed by a return to eighteenth- and early-nineteenth-century style – Louis XV, Louis XVI, Consulate, Empire and Directoire – adapted to contemporary taste. The second of the objectives in forming a new style was to abolish the curve, which had been used as a primary mode of expression in Art Nouveau furniture. Disciplined, stylised bouquets replaced the whiplash stems of Art Nouveau.

New organisations were established in France during the first decade of the twentieth century to enable designers of decorative objects to exhibit their work at regular intervals. The most important of these was the Société des Artistes Décorateurs, formed in 1901. The founding members of the Société des Artistes Décorateurs included prominent designers and architects from the Art Nouveau era, including Eugène Grasset, Hector Guimard and Eugène Gaillard, in addition to individuals who emerged as leaders of the Art Deco movement: Emile Decoeur, Francis Jourdain, Maurice Dufràne, Paul Follot and Pierre Chareau.

Right: A highly stylised two-panel screen of lacquered wood created by Léon Jallot in 1928.

FURNITURE DESIGN IN TRANSITION

Other major designers during these transitional years were Léon Jallot, Paul Iribe (who was to spend a considerable period in the United States), Louis Majorelle, Mathieu Gallerey, Pierre and Tony Selmersheim, Charles Plumet, Théodore Lambert and Henri Bellery-Desfontaines. Their work can be considered as a somewhat modified and simplified version of Art Nouveau, in which increasingly angular compositions were lightly adorned with carved motifs. A bookcase exhibited by Jallot at the 1908 salon provides a typical example of the changing style, its simple form incorporating a curvilinear apron.

THE EMERGENCE OF ART DECO

Further ornamentation was provided by an upper row of panels naturalistically carved in a restrained Belle Epoque manner. However, the veneers were rich and varied, in anticipation of the coming 1920s' style. In 1912, Follot presented a suite of dining-room furniture at the Salon d'Automne in which the chairs and commode were enhanced with pierced baskets of flowers that appear today as high Art Deco – that is, from the mid-1920s rather than the pre-war years. Ruhlmann incorporated the same stylised motif, with modifications, in his celebrated *encoignure* of 1916, indicating that the Art Deco style in furniture would have

Above left: a group of two rosewood bergère *armchairs and two matching* boudoir *chairs in the style of Paul Follet.*

Left: this petite commode *by Paul Iribe dates to 1912, and was one of the pieces commissioned by Jacques Doucet.*

reached maturity by 1920 if not for the unavoidable hiatus caused by World War I.

Two important events occurred during these pre-war years to influence the evolution of the Art Deco style in furniture. In 1909 the Ballets Russes, directed by Diaghilev, opened in Paris. The sets, designed by Léon Bakst, were brilliantly coloured, with bold patterns. These sets, coupled with the savage colours of the Fauves, who exhibited at the 1905 Salon d'Automne, helped interior designers move away from the restrained palettes of the previous era, and to incorporate an unprecedented brilliance in their schemes. Radiant reds and greens were used for cushions, and bold abstract and figural patterns for upholstery, draperies and wallpapers.

THE SALON D'AUTOMNE

The 1910 Salon d'Automne was also extremely important to the development of the coming Modernist style in France. It was at this exhibition that an invitation was extended by the exhibition's jury to the Munich Deutscher Werkbund in the hope that German participation would shake French designers and manufacturers out of the lethargy apparent in their recent work. The Munich exhibit – represented by the work of Thedor Veil, Adalbert Niemeyer, Paul Wenz, Richard Riemerschmid, Otto Baur, Karl Bertsch and Richard Berndl, among others – was intended to inspire the Germans' French counterparts to develop a new and distinctive national style.

Although French cabinetmakers and designers had by 1910 rejected the organic protrusions on Art Nouveau furniture in

Left: Rose Adler designed this table of ebony, sharkskin, metal and enamel for couturier Jacques Doucet in 1926.

Left: a five-piece giltwood and Beauvais tapestry drawing-room suite by French designer Maurice Dufrêne.

Below: a massive, pallissander-veneered bar inlaid with mother of pearl and various stained woods. It is attributed to Jules Leleu, who favoured such floral designs.

favour of a more restrained and functional style, they were not prepared to forego the Belle Epoque's preoccupation with lavish materials. Exotic woods, such as Macassar ebony, rosewood and amboyna, became fashionable, often veneered in patterns that accentuated their contrasting textures. Distinctive grains, such as those found in burl maple and calamander, added to the aura of opulence sought.

FURNITURE EMBELLISHMENT
For large surface areas, designers embellished and sometimes even entirely covered furniture with such exotic materials as mother of pearl, sharkskin (known as shagreen and *galuchat*), parchment, snakeskin, gold and silver leaf, crushed-eggshell lacquer and ivory. These might form a pattern – usually stylised flowers or a geometric motif – or they might take advantage of the nature of the substance itself, perhaps using the imbrication pattern of the shark's skin decoratively. The shapes of furniture ranged from overtly traditional – eighteenth-century *bureau plats*, petite ladies' desks, *gondole* or *bergère* chairs – to more strikingly *moderne*, severely rectilinear with not a curve in sight.

Right: Emile-Jacques Ruhlmann created this girl's room, which was included in Jean Badovici's Intérieurs Français *in 1925.*

Other readily identifiable Modernist images, such as the sunburst, zigzag and chevron, likewise made their entry into the new grammar of decorative ornament before and during World War I in the work of André Mare and Louis Süe, two Parisian interior designers who formed a partnership in 1919. The period was characterised by experimentation, as artists and furniture designers searched for a means to distance themselves from the *fin de siècle* and to create a bona-fide twentieth-century style. In this, neo-classicism became a unifying force.

DEVELOPING TRENDS

Indeed, when viewed retrospectively, there were two distinct trends within Art Deco furniture design. On the one hand, there were the early experiments in what we have now come to recognise as modern furniture, using metals and plastics in forms which could lead to eventual mass production, and on the other the high-quality craftsmanship of which Emile-Jacques Ruhlmann was the greatest exponent. An almost limitless number of French designers applied themselves to the Modernist style. For simplification, the furniture designers of the period can be grouped loosely into three broad categories: traditionalists, Modernists and individualists.

THE TRADITIONALISTS

The traditionalists took France's eighteenth- and early-nineteenth-century cabinet-making heritage as their point of departure . This unimpeachable legacy provided the inspiration for a host of 1920s' designers, most importantly:

Emile-Jacques Ruhlmann, Paul Follot, André Groult, Jules Leleu, Louis Süe and André Mare, Armand-Albert Rateau, Jean-Michel Frank, Henri Rapin, Maurice Dufràne, Léon and Maurice Jallot, Eric Bagge, Georges de Bardyère, Gabriel Englinger, Fernand Nathan, Jean Pascaud, René Gabriel, Marcel Guillemard, Suzanne Guiguichon, Blanch-J Klotz, Lucie Renaudot, Charlotte Chaucet-Guilleré, Georges Renouvin, Pierre Lahalle and Georges Levard, Auguste-Victor Fabre, Pierre-Paul Montagnac, Alfred Porteneuve and the ageing 1900 *maître*, Louis Majorelle. In addition, most of the cabinet-makers in Paris's furniture-making quarter, the Faubourg Saint-Antoine, generated a range of proven, rather traditional, models. Mercier Frères and Saddier et fils produced some good-quality furniture

Left: a chiffonier created in around 1926 by Emile-Jacques Ruhlmann. Veneered in amboyna, the inlaid pattern is of ivory.

Below: a decorated cabinet bombe *in the* Japoniste *style by Clément Mère, a partner in the Süe and Mare collaboration.*

in the modern idiom, as did André Frechet at the Ecole Boulle.

The achievement of the traditionalists was to re-evaluate the traditional furniture styles, take the best and subtly alter and revamp them. Many of the people responsible for furniture design were not themselves great craftsmen, but they were capable of running large workshops and using the talents of their own and other studios' craftsmen to best effect. They were virtuoso performers and they showed off their abilities to the utmost.

EMILE-JACQUES RUHLMANN

Emile-Jacques Ruhlmann (1879-1933) was without peer as a cabinet-maker. A strict traditionalist, his forms were elegant, refined and – above all – simple and sleekly modern in their decoration and detail. His cabinets, desks, tables and chairs were veneered in costly, warm woods, such as amaranth, amboyna, ebony and violet wood, and embellished with silk tassels and subtle touches of ivory in dentate, dotted or diamond patterns. The long, slender legs – sometimes torpedo shaped with cut facets – were often capped with metal *sabots*, or shoes, a concept that was both decorative and practical.

The 1925 Exposition catapulted Ruhlmann to the front of the modern French decorative-arts movement. Until then, he had been known only to an exclusive and wealthy clientele. His pavilion at the Exposition, L'Hôtel du Collectionneur, would change that, however. Hundreds of thousands of visitors flocked through its monumental doors to gaze in awe at the majestic interior. Ruhlmann reacted with remarkable equanimity to the post-1925 advent of metal into furniture design, in view of the fact that much of his great reputation rested on the use of sumptuous veneers. He

Above: this lacquered and silver-leafed pirogue *(canoe) sofa was made in around 1919–20 by designer Eileen Gray.*

Right: a bench created by Eileen Gray from in around 1923. The model was made in various woods.

adjusted bravely to metal's advances, incorporating chrome and silvered metal into his designs, when many of his furniture forms became quite rectilinear; at the same time, his ivory dots and silk fringes gave way to chrome fittings, leather cushions and swivel bases.

Many of Ruhlmann's contemporaries generated superior furniture. Among the finest were Süe et Mare, whom Jean Badovici described as 'an admirable association of two dissimilar minds which combined the best of their qualities to put them at the service of Beauty. One provides a sure and precise knowledge and a rigorous sense of geometry; the other a refined and delicate sensibility'. The result was a highly distinctive and lavish range of furnishings inspired by the Louis XIV, Louis XV, *Restauration* and Louis-Philippe periods.

THE MODERNISTS

The Modernists rebelled against the tightness of the neo-classical harness, bringing their own blend of individualism – defiant or understated – to the projects at hand. For these, metal was *de rigueur*. The most notable modernists were Jacques Adnet, Edouard-Joseph Djo-Bourgeois, André-Leon Arbus, Robert Block, Pierre Petit, René Prou, Louis Sognot, Charlotte Alix, Michel Dufet, Maurice Barret, Léon Bouchet, Georges Champion, Renée Kinsbourg, Maurice Matet and Paul Dupré-Lafon. These were joined towards 1930 by architects, who moved increasingly into the field of furniture design. René Herbst, Robert Mallet-Stevens, Jean Burkhalter, Pierre Chareau, André Luráat, Le Corbusier, Charlotte Perriand and Jean-Charles Moreux – to name only the most prominent – extended their architectural designs to the building's interior space and furnishings, giving prestige and authority to the Modernist philosophy. Le Corbusier's best-known furniture pieces, for

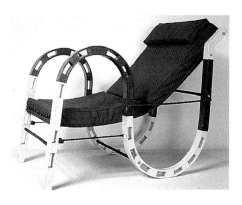

Above: this wood and canvas armchair dates from around 1938 and was designed by the versatile Eileen Gray.

Left: Pierre Legrain and Jean Dunand collaborated on this red-lacquered cabinet commissioned by Jacques Doucet.

Right: a jungle confrontation is depicted on a lacquer and ivory screen by Jean Dunand from a design by Paul Jouave.

Below: a table by Jean Dunand. Red lacquer squares embellish the table; note the mass of coquille d'oeuf *on the top.*

example, are his chaise-longues and chairs, often fashioned of tubular-steel frames and with simple but comfortable leather seats, designed in collaboration with his cousin Pierre Jeanneret and Charlotte Perriand.

The third group of furniture designers, that of the individualist, relates to those individuals whose brilliance and range of influences defy ready categorisation. Only four qualify: Pierre Legrain, with his bizarre blend of tribal African and Modernist influences; Irish-born Eileen Gray, with her lacquered Orientalism, whimsy, theatricality and Modernism; Eugène Printz, whose distinctly personal and kinetic designs were constructed in the traditional manner; and Marcel Coard, whose innovative spirit was allowed only an infrequent escape from the bulk of his more traditional and constrained decorating commissions.

EILEEN GRAY

Eileen Gray (1879-1933) started out fashioning exquisite handmade objects, such as screens, tables and chairs. These were often embellished with Japanese lacquer, whose technique she studied with the master, Sougawara. Eventually she moved on to more rectilinear and strongly functional furniture, as well as to architecture. For *modiste* Suzanne Talbot she designed a Paris apartment between 1919 and 1920 which included a canoe-shaped chaise-longue in patinated bronze lacquer with subtle scalloped edges and a base comprising 12 rounded arches. By 1927, however, her chair designs were radically different and distinctly *moderne*. A padded-leather-seat *Transat* armchair, set on a rigid lacquer frame with chromed-steel connecting elements, was more akin to Le Corbusier than to Ruhlmann *et al*. Her case pieces, with built-in cupboards that feature swivelling drawers and doors set on tracks, and tables that moved easily on wheels, were considerably more practical.

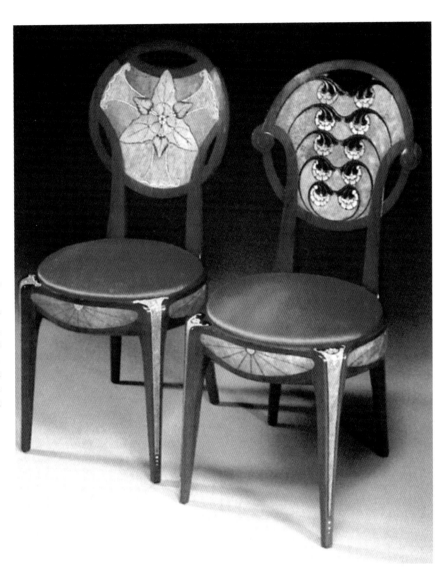

Left: an occasional table by Clément Rousseau in exotic woods, shagreen, ivory and mother of pearl, c.1921.

Above: a pair of chairs by Clément Rousseau. Their frames are rosewood, their predominant material sharkskin.

Right: The elegant surface of this table by Pierre Chareau dating from around 1928 comprises palissander-wood veneer and an etched-glass top. Note the horizontal and vertical directions of the veneer.

Pierre Legrain (1887-1929) initially made his mark as a designer of book covers for his wealthy patron Jacques Doucet. One of his most famous pieces of furniture was the *Zebra* chair, or chaise-longue. His clear affinity with all things African could hardly have been made more explicit than in this piece made in 1925. Compared to such representations of the opposite extreme of Art Deco as Eileen Gray's experiments in metals, Legrain's is nothing short of bizarre. The zebra skin is imitated in velvet, the armrest is decorated on the reverse with abstract patterns expensively executed in mother of pearl. The arm rest is left open from the front in order to house a small shelf whose purpose could be nothing more than aesthetic. The overall design is almost crude, appearing both clumsy and uncomfortable, but

exudes a sensuous feeling of gratuitous luxury and decadence.

Among other important furniture designers in Paris was Jean Dunand (1877-1942), who mixed traditional lacquerwork with modern, angular forms. He was known for his *dinanderie* (the art of chasing and hammering metal) and for his lacquerwork, and also designed and decorated elaborate furniture, including cabinets, panels and screens. Indeed, lacquer exponents tended to concentrate their production on screens and *panneaux décoratifs*; for example, Gaston Suisse, Gaston Priou and Katsu Hamanaka. Dunand's pieces were often covered with figural or animal designs, either by Dunand himself or after a noted artist.

Dunand's pieces themselves may have been designed by an *ébéniste* such as

Ruhlmann. His huge screens, often made of silver, gold and black lacquer, displayed huge geometric motifs, exotic Oriental or African maidens, lush landscapes or elaborate mythological scenes. His most famous piece was a bed made in 1930 for Mme Bertholet, in lacquer and mother of pearl.

ROUSSEAU AND CHANAUX

Two artisans emerged as masters of Modernist materials. The first was Clément Rousseau, who designed and executed finely detailed furniture and precious objects in rare woods, toiled and stained leather, carved ivory and enamel. The other was Adolphe Chanaux, a virtuoso craftsman who executed furniture designs for André Groult, Emile-Jacques Ruhlmann and Jean-Michel Frank, as well as for his own creations. Chanaux's importance lay in his mastery of all of the period's most exotic and fashionable furniture materials – sharkskin, parchment, vellum, ivory, straw marquetry and hand-sewn leather – to which he applied his talents with equal facility.

In summary, no unified furniture aesthetic had emerged at the 1925 Paris Exposition. Rather, there was an uneasy coexistence of contradictory images and styles. Varnished rosewood appeared alongside tubular nickelled or chrome steel; the Cubist rose competed with Constructionist geometry; and the brilliant colours derived from the Ballets Russes and the Fauves clashed with the subdued tints used by Modernists who preferred achromatism.

Just as there had been a transitional period between the Art Nouveau and Art Deco periods, so there was a gradual progression from high-style Art Deco to Modernism during the late 1920s.

THE UNION DES ARTISTES MODERNES

In 1930, a new organisation was formed to give identity to the group of designers who took Modernism as their doctrine: the Union des Artistes Modernes (UAM). Members included René Herbst, Francis Jourdain, Hélène Henri, Robert Mallet-Stevens, Pierre Chareau, Raymond Templier, Edouard-Joseph Djo-Bourgeois, Eileen Gray, Le Corbusier and Charlotte Perriand. These Modernist architects

and designers rejected the ornamentation characteristic of the early 1920s, giving priority to function over form. They designed furniture in materials such as steel, chrome and painted-metal tubes, in which individual elements were designed for mass production.

INDUSTRIAL MATERIALS

As simplicity became increasingly fashionable, furniture designers working in the high Art Deco style had to combine their traditional forms with industrial methods and materials. In glass, René Lalique extended the traditional uses of the medium in his designs for a series of tables and consoles. Wrought iron was another material used in furniture manufacture

Left: the dining table and chairs are of glass and chromed metal. The table features inlaid panels by René Lalique.

Right: this elegant and luxurious bathroom was designed by Armand-Albert Rateau for Jeanne Lanvin between 1920 and 1922.

during the 1920s by such leading proponents as Edgar Brandt, Raymond Subes, Michel and Jules Nics, Paul Kiss, Adelbert Szabo and Richard Desvallières. By the end of the decade, wood had practically disappeared from the furniture shown at the annual salons. The glorious age of France's *ébénistes* had passed.

JACQUES DOUCET'S PATRONAGE

The first patron of the new Modernist style was the couturier Jacques Doucet, who in 1912 commissioned Paul Iribe to design and furnish his new apartment on the Avenue du Bois, Paris. Doucet sold his collection of eighteenth-century furniture and *objets d'art* at auction, replacing it with contemporary paintings and furnishings. In the same year, Paul Poiret, also well known as a fashion designer, established his Atelier Martine. In 1924, Doucet again sought Modernist designers to decorate the studio which he had commissioned the architect Paul Ruau to design for him in Neuilly to house his collection of Oceanic and African art. Pierre Legrain, who had worked for Paul Iribe during Doucet's earlier commission, was joined in Neuilly by a cross-section of Paris' most avant-garde artist-designers: Eileen Gray, Marcel Coard, André Groult, Rose Adler, Constantin Brancusi, Paul Mergier and also Louis Marcoussis.

Another celebrated couturière and art patron, Jeanne Lanvin, retained Armand-Albert Rateau to decorate her house and boutique, and Madeleine Vionnet commissioned Jean Dunand similarly to furnish her house with his lacquered furniture. His patinated-bronze, wood and marble furnishings were rife with elaborate floral and animal motifs – birds supporting a bronze coffee table; deer amid foliage on a bathroom bas-relief; marguerites entwining a dressing table. While Rateau's furniture and overall vision are among the most figurative and truly sculptural of the period, the heavily veneered, embellished and/or lacquered pieces of many of the others are much more handsome and restrained, often deriving from classical shapes. Classical scrolls, or *volutes*, were used to decorate furniture, as well as stylised wings, animals, birds and human figures.

THE PARISIAN DEPARTMENT STORES

Expensive and élitist as the luxury trade undoubtedly was, its resurgence depended on other factors. Apart from a few specialist shops, the outlet for contemporary furniture was limited. When the new department stores realised that design could be of great use to them, the situation altered.

During the inter-war years, Paris home-owners could select their furniture from four major department stores – Au Printemps, Le Louvre, Au Bon Marché and Les Galeries Lafayette. A fifth, Trois Quartiers, was established in 1929. The function of these stores was that of arbiter of taste, especially in the promotion of modern household

commodities. To serve their clients better, the stores established their own art studios in which to design and manufacture what they believed the customers wanted, rather than what they had previously been forced to accept through lack of choice. The studio for Au Printemps was Primavera; that of Le Louvre, Studium Louvre; that of Au Bon Marché, Pomone; and that of Les Galeries Lafayette, La Maîtrise. The cream of France's young designers – Louis Sognot, René Prou, Robert Block and Etienne Kohlmann – were brought in to direct these studios and modern furniture production. The public was easily persuaded that it was, at long last, getting what it wanted: modern furniture at a reasonable price.

Competition between the department stores spread to smaller firms, such as René Joubert and Philippe Petit's Décoration Intérieure

Below: a bizarre bronze and marble table by Armand-Albert Rateau, with four stylised birds used as supports.

Right: a design for a young man's bedroom by M Guillemard, furnished by Primavera.

Below: a DIM jewellery cabinet decorated with Chinese red lacquer and coquille d'oeuf, *1926.*

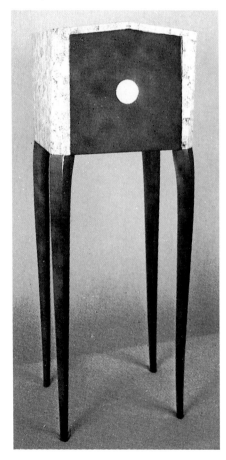

Moderne (DIM); André Domin and Marcel Genevrière's Dominique; Michel Dufet's Meubles Artistiques Modernes (MAM); and Louis Süe and André Mare's La Compagnie des Arts Français. Furniture benefited from the competition, as designs and materials were modernised. At the 1925 Exposition, both the stores and firms were well placed to present a wide range of ultra-modern household goods to the public.

ART DECO FURNITURE REASSESSED

Art Deco furniture is certainly one of the most interesting and inspired applications of the style. The high prices it commands nowadays are certainly due to its rarity, but they also reflect another factor: that of the value of quality craftsmanship. Even when Ruhlmann sold his furniture during the 1920s, such pieces were only affordable by the wealthiest of wealthy clients. If his work commanded high prices, it was not because of commercial greed but because of the months of skilled labour and the use of the most expensive materials as expressions of his genius. If such a piece of furniture were to be copied today, it would be next to impossible to find a cabinet-maker who would be capable of producing it. The 1920s and 1930s witnessed, among so many things, the dying of the old crafts.

NON-GALLIC
ART DECO
FURNITURE

By the end of the 1920s, much tubular-steel furniture was being created both by architects and furniture designers. The public was asked to reconsider the aesthetic merits of utilitarian, even humble materials, such as steel and metal alloys, for furniture production. Metal entered the home through the kitchen door – in the traditional manufacture of metal household utensils – after which it gradually worked its way into the other rooms of the house. Final and complete acceptance came in the selection of metal rather than wood for salon and dining-room furniture. In between the elegantly carved and veneered confections of high-style Art Deco and the near-antithetical, ultra-*moderne* tubular-steel and leather creations of Le Corbusier and others were myriad pieces of furniture designed by Europeans that reflected either – at times even both – of the Art Deco design schools, with the occasional unique and completely innovative design making its own waves.

Preceding page: De Stijl designer Gerrit Rietveld's Red and Blue Chair *of 1918 has become an icon of modern design.*

Above: A living-room suite designed by Félix Del Marle in 1926 for 'Madame B'.

The infiltration of Modernist furniture into the home and office was not just restricted to France. It had, in fact, developed more quickly in more progressive countries. Germany is often considered the pioneering nation in the development of the modern movement. The Belgian designer Henry van der Velde founded the Weimar School of Applied Arts in 1906, which was absorbed in 1919 by Walter Gropius who, in turn, founded the Bauhaus. This was an attempt to unify all the myriad of disciplines within the decorative arts under the general direction of architecture.

THE BAUHAUS

The Bauhaus instructors and their students advocated rational and functional design, and an increased dependence on the machine for mass-production. One of the most important Bauhaus furniture designers was Marcel Breuer who, with Mart Stam and Ludwig Mies van der Rohe, was the first developer of the

cantilevered tubular-metal chair. Later, in England, Breuer explored further the use of industrial materials in his design for a laminated plywood lounge chair, manufactured by the Isokon Furniture Company in London.

THE PRAZSKE UMELECKE DILNY
New developments in Eastern Europe reflected a similar adherence to the new Modernist philosophy. In Prague, the Prazske Umelecke Dilny (Prague Art Shop) had been founded in

1912. Leaders of this school included Pavel Janak, Josef Chocol, Vlatislav Hofman and Josef Gocar, who designed furniture inspired by the Cubism of Braque and Picasso, and some of whom believed that only a designer's artistic concepts were important, and that technical and functional aspects of design were secondary. The outbreak of World War I put an end to the endeavour.

Although most critics view German design of the 1920s in the context of the Modernism

Above: the Finnish architect and designer Alvar Aalto created this bent, laminated wood chair and blocky sideboard.

Right: the Russian-born architect/designer Serge Chermayeff designed this walnut- and coromandel-veneered sideboard while working for the British furniture-makers Waring & Gillow.

Below: a British coffee table, c.1930, veneered with peach-coloured mirror glass.

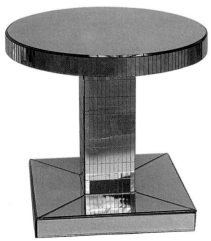

embodied by the Bauhaus, many German designers now considered Modernists actually created furniture in the contemporary French style. Bruno Paul, of the Munich Vereinigte Werkstätten and director of the Berlin Kunstgewerbeschule, for example, invariably incorporated an element of richness into his furniture designs. He tried to update German Baroque traditions, and while his veneered pieces were often embellished with ivory knobs and finials like Ruhlmann's, his forms were more awkward and less sleek, the legs more serpentine than gently tapering. Well into the 1920s, he continued to design pieces in luxurious materials and with thick, glossy veneers for the Deutscher Werkbund, a group known

for its emphasis on the union of artists and industry. The furniture designed by Paul for the 1927 Cologne Exhibition was more in keeping with the Modernist high style in Paris than the machine ethics of the Bauhaus.

VENEERING AND FINISHING

German designers like Bruno Paul thus made expensive, custom-made furniture in limited quantities. According to one contemporary commentator, 'Special attention is paid here to the wood used and to the finish. The simpler and more severe the piece the more attention is paid to the materials. Especially handsome inlaid pieces are preferred because it is possible by clever assembling of veneers to achieve beautiful patterns'. That observation drew an obvious comparison with the well-crafted and sumptuous cabinetry of France's foremost designers, such as Ruhlmann and Leleu, who also catered to an elite clientele.

DE STIJL

In The Netherlands, the de Stijl group was formed in 1917. Theo van Doesburg, Gerrit Rietveld and Félix Del Marle designed furniture intended to fill the Utopian interior spaces conceived by the leaders of the movement, Piet Mondrian and van Doesburg. Their furniture was angular and skeletal, of simple construction, employing planar, wooden boards painted either black or in the primary colours favoured by de Stijl artists. Architect-

designer Gerrit Rietveld created his famous *Rood Blauwe Stoel* (*Red and Blue Chair*) in 1918. Just as the de Stijl movement's painters combined simple geometric shapes, primary colours and horizontal and vertical lines in their canvases, so this classic chair combined these same primary ingredients in a three-dimensional manner; the final result may have been uncomfortable, but it has none the less become an icon of modern design.

SCANDINAVIAN FURNITURE

French-inspired furniture was also produced in Scandinavia, and by the late 1920s the functionalism championed by the Bauhaus had begun to assert itself. This influence was felt the most strongly in Sweden, which was more

Above: an elegant chaise-longue designed by Betty Joel, a proponent of functional and easy-to-care-for furniture.

Left: Sir Edward Maufe designed this desk for the 1925 Paris Exhibition. It is made of champhor, mahogany and gilded ebony.

receptive to avant-garde German ideology than its neighbours. Erik Gunnar Asplund was perhaps the premier Scandinavian designer to work in the Modernist style. He designed an armchair made of mahogany, leather and ivory in around 1925, produced by David Blomberg of Stockholm, in a style which evoked the Paris fashion. The chair was part of a suite of furniture favourably reviewed by the critics at the 1925 Exposition.

Some of the Bauhaus' most fruitful and artistic ideas were evident in furniture shown at the landmark 1930 Stockholm Exhibition held at the Nordiska Kompaniet (NK) department store. The exhibition revealed a revolutionary attitude to domestic design, with special emphasis on residential architecture and furnishings. In keeping with modern concerns for practicality, flexibility and hygiene, dwellings at the exhibition had large windows, light walls and a minimum of furnishings. The furniture was geometrical in shape and extremely light, with restrained decoration.

BRUNO MATHSSON

The new furniture forms developed by the Bauhaus architects had a profound impact on international design by the 1930s. Noteworthy were Breuer's bent tubular-steel models, which were imitated, albeit with modifications, throughout Europe. In Scandinavia, however, designers preferred to incorporate Breuer's functionalism with traditional materials, such as wood, in serial production. Bruno Mathsson is probably the best-known Swedish designer of the period. One of his notable furniture

Right: this lavish table and chairs were created by Joseph Urban in around 1921.

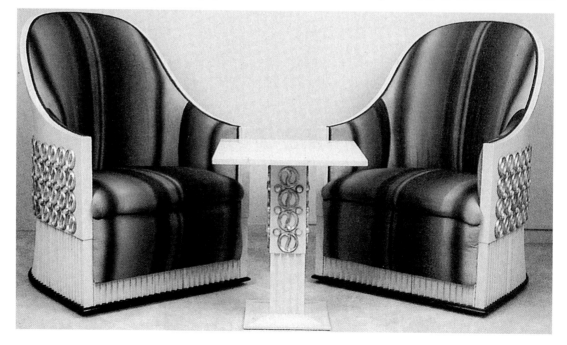

designs was the *Eva* chair of 1934, produced by the Firma Karl Mathsson in Varnamo. Made of bent beech upholstered in woven fabric, the model was sculpturally moulded to fit the human body. Mathsson's experiments in bent and laminated wood, also combined with his studies of function and maximum comfort, generated many popular designs which have remained in continuous production since their conception several decades ago.

DANISH DESIGNERS

At the same time, designers in Denmark moved into new areas of experimentation. Kaare Klint made furniture which combined practicality with economy. His first independent commission was to design exhibition cases and seats for the Thorwaldsen Museum of Decorative Arts in Copenhagen. His *Red Chair*, designed in 1927 for the museum, was widely acclaimed.

Alvar Aalto began to design modern furniture during the 1920s. His *Scroll* or *Paimio* armchair of around 1929 has become a classic of modern Finnish design. The frame and seat are made of laminated and painted bentwood. The model captures the qualities of functionalism and lightness sought in tubular-metal furniture, adding a pleasing note of grace in its use of natural wood and sinuous curves. Aalto's bent- and laminated-wood stacking stools of 1930-33, produced by Korhonen in Turku, were also very successful commercially due to their formal simplicity and inexpensiveness. The stools have remained entirely practical and adaptable to multiple requirements in the variants produced later.

DESIGNERS IN STEEL

Other Scandinavian designers also experimented with tubular steel. In 1929, Herman

Left: Paul T Frankl's Skyscraper *bookcase/cabinet, made from birch and lacquer in about 1928. Frankl was the first US designer to embrace the skyscraper as a decorative motif.*

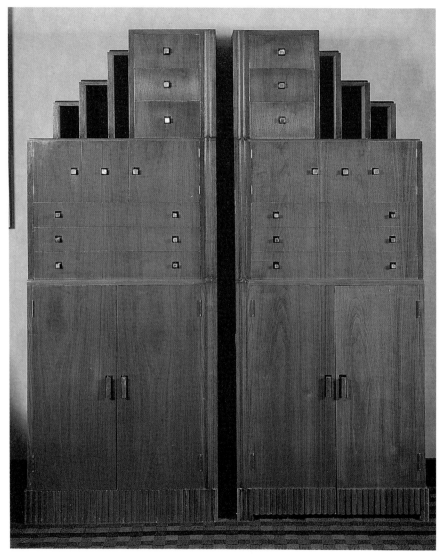

Above: two 'skyscraper' chests of drawers made of ebony-trimmed walnut designed by Paul T Frankl, c.1928.

Munthe-Kaas of Norway designed an armchair produced by the Christiania Jernsengfabrikk of Oslo. Although its form is based on Breuer's tubular-steel prototype, the model differs in its incorporation of an unusual metal-strap back and a series of simple string hooks that support the upholstered seat.

BRITISH FURNITURE

In Britain, which had a strong native tradition of solid Arts and Crafts-style furniture, craftsmen such as Edward Barnsley designed rectilinear, sturdy pieces that bore no similarity whatsoever to *moderne* continental designs. Others, however, such as Betty Joel, Ambrose Heal, the Russian-born Serge Ivan Chermayeff, Gordon Russell and the design firm PEL (Practical Equipment Limited) produced functionalist furniture with distinctly modern lines and – especially in the case of Chermayeff – occasional stylised-floral pieces. Chermayeff, who trained initially as an artist in Paris, has been credited with the introduction of the modern movement into Britain. His chromium-plated metal tubular furniture and unit storage systems represented a dramatic departure from the sterile, tradition-bound models of his adopted country.

THE INFLUENCE OF JOHN ROGERS

Along with Chermayeff, the designer John C Rogers was instrumental in bringing the modern style to England. In an article in the *DIA Journal*, Rogers had begun as early as 1914 to instil a new spirit of design into British industry. He pleaded for a national conversion to Modernism and for a final rejection of the Arts and Crafts philosophy. In 1931, he visited the Bauhaus in Dessau with Jack Pritchard and Wells Coates, a trip which inspired the furniture he exhibited at Dorland

Hall, London, two years later. In 1932, in collaboration with Raymond McGrath and Coates, Rogers redesigned the interior of the BBC; he later emigrated to the United States. Coates also designed modern furniture during the 1930s for PEL, including notably an ebonised-wood and chromium-plated metal desk inspired by an earlier Breuer model.

THE INFILTRATION OF THE AVANT-GARDE

The general absence of furniture in England in the Modernist style was thus punctuated by a handful of spirited avant-garde models. Sir Edward Maufe, an architect known principally for Guildford Cathedral, designed a range of furniture that appears to have been inspired by Paris. A typical example is provided by a desk manufactured by W Rowcliffe in around 1924, exhibited at the 1925 Exposition. Made of mahogany, camphor and ebony gessoed and gilded with white gold, the desk had all the sumptuousness and ostentation characteristic of prominent French models.

Russell designed a boot cupboard in 1925 in Honduras mahogany in a style very similar to French models introduced a few years earlier. And in 1929 Heal produced a desk and chair in weathered oak on which the perpendicular detailing again betrayed the influence of contemporary continental models.

BETTY JOEL

At the end of World War I Betty Joel and her husband established their decorating firm in South Hayling, with a showroom in Sloane Street in London. Early designs revealed the fact that she was self-taught. By the end of

Right: Paul T Frankl's man's cabinet and mirror, c.1938. Silver- and gold-plated metal half moons enhance the doors.

the 1920s, however, she had developed a distinctive furniture style in which curved contours (described by her as silhouettes of the female form) predominated. Superfluous mouldings and projections were eliminated; ornamentation was achieved through a range of luxurious, contrasting veneers.

Joel's firm won many commissions to decorate libraries, boardrooms, shops and hotels, and many of her designs were popularised by English manufacturers of modestly priced furnishings. She retired in 1937 and is primarily remembered today for an inexpensive line of furniture aimed at the working woman.

THE UNITED STATES

Although Paris was across the Atlantic, it was

Below: a red-lacquered 'puzzle' desk, embellished with silver, by Paul T Frankl.

not too far for its influence to be felt in the United States. American designers were well aware of the prevailing Modernist style in Paris through periodicals of the day, and through a succession of exhibitions that travelled across the country during the second half of the 1920s. A loan exhibition of items from the 1925 Exposition opened at the Museum of Fine Arts, Boston, in January 1926, from where it proceeded to the Metropolitan Museum of Art, New York, and six other American cities.

THE FRENCH INFLUENCE

Correspondingly, attempts were occasionally made to introduce a flamboyant European style of furniture, some noteworthy. The Company of Mastercraftsmen in New York, for example, produced shameless copies of contemporary French models, replete with marquetry panels and ivory trim. Joseph Urban, an Austrian architect better known as a designer of stage and cinema sets, likewise designed somewhat theatrical furniture, such as a table and armchair, made around 1920, both of classical proportions and adorned with mother-of-pearl inlays, manufactured by the Mallin Furniture Factory.

AMERICAN MODERNISM

In general, however, the high Parisian style of the 1925 Exposition was rejected by the public, which viewed it as a Gallic eccentricity too exuberant for traditional local tastes. And, when Modernism established itself in America during the late 1920s, it was the strain of northern European machine-made, mass-produced metal furniture which found acceptance.

Paul Frankl, whose 1930 cry 'Ornament = crime' was taken up by a good many *moderne* American designers, is known primarily for his skyscraper furniture, inspired by the

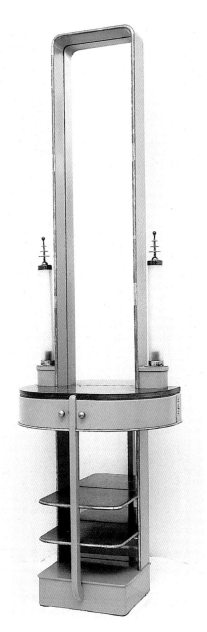

Left: a side table designed by Kem Weber for the Bissingers. The piece is made of burl walnut, glass, silvered and painted wood, chromium-plated metal, maple and cedar.

Above: an armchair in Macassar ebony by Kem Weber, probably designed for the Kaufmann department store, c.1928.

recesses on the tall buildings which soared above his New York gallery. He also created a man's cabinet and series of 'puzzle' desks that incorporated materials and finishes found on contemporary French models: red and black lacquer, gold- and silver-plated metal, and gold and silver leaf.

SKYSCRAPER STYLE

The German national Karl Emanuel (Kem) Weber and J B Peters, two Los Angeles designers, also adapted the skyscraper style to their tall pieces, and Chicagoan Abel Faidy produced a leather settee with a whimsical design derived from architecture for a private penthouse apartment which could easily have been custom-built for Radio City or the Chrysler Building, or else some equally contemporary complex. Weber was trapped in California at the outbreak of World War I.

Refused permission to return to his homeland, he finally settled in Los Angeles, where he joined the design studio at Barker Bros as a draughtsman. In 1927 he opened his own design studio in Hollywood, listing himself as an industrial designer. Not only was Weber virtually the only decorative-arts designer to embrace the Modernist creed on the West Coast, but his style was highly distinctive. For the John W Bissinger residence in San Francisco Weber created a striking suite of green-painted bedroom furniture enhanced with Hollywood-type decorative metal accents.

FRANK LLOYD WRIGHT

The metal and wood furniture of Frank Lloyd Wright was not as severe as that of the Bauhaus school. For instance, his renowned 1936-39 desk and chair, called *Cherokee Red* and designed for the S C Johnson & Son building in Racine,

Right: Cherokee Red *desk and chair, 1936-39, by Frank Lloyd Wright for S C Johnson & Son.*

Wisconsin, have their steel frames enamelled in a warm, russet-brown tone which complements the American walnut of the chair arms and desk top, as well as the chair's brown-toned upholstery. The two pieces are an essay on the circle, oval and line – and are undoubtedly far more inviting to an office worker than, for example, the shiny chrome-and-black leather pieces of Breuer *et al*.

AN AMERICAN MIXTURE

Eliel Saarinen, Eugene Schoen, Wolfgang Hoffmann (the son of the Viennese Josef Hoffmann, and an American emigrant), Gilbert Rohde and Joseph Urban were among the many designers who applied their talents to creating furniture for the American market. On the whole, their pieces were sturdy, mass-produced and distinctly Modernist, some echoing French, German and Viennese design, others uniquely American in their form, colour and materials. Aluminium, chromium and other metal furniture was in the ascendancy, but the wooden pieces continued to thrive, with veneers of native woods such as holly, birch, burr maple and walnut handsomely covering large surface areas.

ELIEL SAARINEN

One of the finest Modernist furniture designers in the United States was Eliel Saarinen, a native of Finland. For his own house at Michigan's Cranbrook Academy, Saarinen designed a dining-room ensemble which drew on the principles of French Modernist design. The chairs have classically fluted backs emphasised by the contrasting colours of the pale fir veneer and the intersecting black-painted vertical stripes. The accompanying table is inlaid with an elegant geometrical pattern which recalls the restrained parquetry designs

Left: an oak side chair (c.1916-22) designed by Frank Lloyd Wright for the Imperial Hotel in Tokyo.

Right: a vintage photograph of the 'Great Workroom' of the S C Johnson Building in Racine designed by Frank Lloyd Wright. Note the smart desk and chair sets.

introduced by Dominique and DIM in Paris some years earlier.

Eugene Schoen, a native of New York, also created furniture in a restrained Modernist style. After visiting the 1925 Exposition, he established his own interior-decorating firm in Manhattan. Some of his more notable models, manufactured by Schmied, Hungate & Kotzian, betrayed a strong French influence in such details as their Directoire-style sabre legs and fluted backs.

MASS-PRODUCTION

Many designers in the United States created Modernist wood furniture, much of it manufactured in the industry's principal centre, Grand Rapids, Michigan, by firms such as Berkey & Gay, the Johnson-Handley-Johnson Company and the Imperial Furniture Company.

Included were Herman Rosse, Ilonka Karasz, Jules Bouy, Herbert Lippmann, Ely Jacques Kahn, Robert Locher, Winold Reiss and Norman Bel Geddes. Furniture manufacturers like the Herman Miller Furniture Co in Zeeland, Michigan, the Troy Sunshade Co in Troy, Ohio, and the Ypsilanti Reed Furniture Co, in Ionia, Michigan, retained designers such as these to provide them with models for their lines of mass-produced furniture.

DONALD DESKEY

In metal furniture, Donald Deskey emerged as the country's premier designer, combining the luxury of French Modernism with the technology of the Bauhaus. Perhaps one of the finest examples of his work was his dining table for the Abby Rockefeller Milton apartment, between 1933 and 1934. Although the piece included a Macassar-ebony top, it was the inclusion of new materials – polished chrome and glass, and the siting of a bulb beneath the top to provide dramatic lighting effects – that drew the critics' praise.

For his interiors for the Radio City music hall in 1932, Deskey set convention aside in a display of ostentation intended to buoy the Depression-wracked nation seeking refuge in films and live entertainment. The private apartment above the music hall which Deskey designed for its impresario, Roxy Rothafel, was even more lavish.

Several other designers in the United States created excellent metal furniture during the late 1920s and 1930s, in particular Gilbert

Below: an executive suite consisting of a desk, chair and lamps designed for S L Rothafel by Donald Deskey.

Rohde, Wolfgang and Pola Hoffmann, Warren McArthur, Walter Dorwin Teague, and the lighting specialist Walter von Nessen. Walter Kantack, a New York metalware manufacturer, also produced inspired metal pieces of furniture, as did the architect William Lescaze, of Howe and Lescaze.

A GLITZY STYLE

At the far end of the spectrum was T H Robsjohn-Gibbings of California, who worked in a luxurious and fiercely anachronistic neo-classical style which greatly appealed to his wealthy clients in the showbusiness community. Classical motifs such as scrolls, palmettes, lyres, rams ' heads and hoofed feet adorned his tables, mirrors and chairs, pieces which were mostly made of parcel-gilt carved wood and gilt-bronze.

THE ADVENT OF NEW MATERIALS

By the mid-1930s, it was evident that metal had won the battle with wood for the domestic American furniture market. Whereas wood was still preferred in some sectors of the household market, metal increasingly began to win adherents. By then, such synthetic materials as Formica and Lucite were already being used in furniture design, with an armchair by Elsie de Wolfe, in a traditional, scrolled-back design of moulded Lucite, demonstrating a strange but witty meeting of the old and the new.

Left:a side chair created for Hope Hampton by Elsie de Wolfe, c.1939. What makes the chair astonishing is the use of Lucite for the 'traditional' back and legs.

ART DECO
METALWORK

Above: a pair of doors covered in monel metal adorn the lobby of New York's First National City Trust Co.

Right: a slender copper vase created by Jean Dunand, c.1920-25. It has been gilded and patinated.

Preceding page: this bronze grille in the style of Brandt is from the Circle Tower Building, Indianapolis, completed in 1938.

The history of Art Deco metalwork is also that of changing materials. The 1920s was the period of wrought iron, bronze and copper. By the early 1930s, these had not been completely replaced, but designers favoured the more modern aluminium, steel and chrome. Adaptability and inventiveness flourished in Art Deco metalwork. Metal was often used on its own for gates and doors, but it could also be employed in conjunction with almost any of the other favoured materials. The 1930s were remarkable, not only for any single colour preference, but for the lack of any colour at all. Glass and shiny metals complemented each other; both were reflecting and anonymous, sparkling and transparent. The typical 1930s' room had mirrored walls, with discreet metal borders, repeated in the bent-metal furniture. There were no distractions, except for their own reflections. Such stark ideas were a long way from those involved in the initial resurgence of metalwork.

Art Deco metalwork pieces ranged from the intimacy of a commemorative medallion or a small mantelpiece clock to the huge entrance gates for the 1925 Exposition. As wrought iron has few limitations beyond that of the craftsman's skill, it broke through the confines of use in one specific area. New developments in technology made wrought iron indispensable where any type of scientific innovation introduced into the home or building required decorative camouflage. Radiators cried out to be covered, and wrought iron was ideal for this purpose because it neither obstructed the flow of heated air, nor was it adversely affected by it. Lift cages became decorative focuses in building lobbies, co-ordinated in design with railings and entrance doors to create an overall unity that was modern, practical and stunning in its impact. The combination of wrought iron with other metals, such as copper, silver, bronze, steel and aluminium expanded the opportunities for memorable, dramatic and unusual decorative effects.

SUBJECT MATTER IN METALWORK

In general, the Art Deco movement was broadly defined by two predominant styles. The first and most strongly 'traditional' made use of stylisations of nature: of birds, flowers and animals; natural phenomena such as clouds, waterfalls and sunbursts were also subject to varying degrees of geometrification. An almost Mannerist elongation of proportions and an exaggeration of round volumes were also much in evidence, and there was a predilection for choosing those animals and plants as subjects that naturally exhibited some of these qualities. Greyhounds, gazelles, pigeons and ripe fruit were among the motifs that came to be associated with Art Deco style. After 1925, wrought iron also began to reflect in its images the more simplified geometric lines of the 'rationalists', as well as the sleek lines of machinery, aeroplanes and steamships. The beauty of the straight line had thus become the new aesthetic.

THE DOMINANCE OF PARIS

Art Deco metalwork was dominated by Parisian designers, notably Edgar Brandt, Jean Dunand and Jean Puiforcat. They worked in three entirely different manners, however, each producing a distinctive metalwork style which inspired designers in France, the rest of Europe and the United States.

JEAN DUNAND AND JEAN PUIFORCAT

Jean Dunand (1877-1942) was a designer *extraordinaire* who trained first as a sculptor. He directed his talents to various mediums, but finally made his name in lacquerwork, applying the coloured resin to wood and metal surfaces and creating jewellery, bookbindings, vases, tables, panels, screens and mantelpieces of the utmost beauty. Jean Puiforcat (1897-1945) also worked in metal, and his stunning creations in silver and silver-gilt, often with semi-precious stone and glass embellishments, occupy a unique place in Art Deco design.

THE FRENCH STYLE

Other French metalworkers included Raymond Subes, Paul Kiss, Armand-Albert Rateau, Louis Sognot and Nics Frères. Their console tables, lighting fixtures, grilles, doors and screens were beautifully executed and featured various motifs from the Art Deco repertory. Pierre-Paul Montagnac and Gaston-Etienne le Bourgeois, a painter and sculptor respective-ly, successfully allied modernity and tradition in wrought-iron design. But in the end it was Brandt's *oeuvre* that set the standard, not only

Left: a chrome hatstand in the shape of a woman's head by the Italian designer Bozzi. Note the Marcel-waved hairstyle which fixes it irrevocably in the 1930s' era.

Right: a pair of andirons crafted in wrought iron by Edgar Brandt during the early 1920s, when the serpent was a popular decorative motif.

Below: this lift door, 1927-28, once adorned Selfridge's store in London. Edgar Brandt designed the wrought-iron and bronze panel.

for French, but also for other European and American ironwork as well.

EDGAR BRANDT

Brandt (1880-1960) was an ironworker of immense talent and breadth who created jewellery, vases, lamps and firedogs, as well as grilles, doors, panels and screens. He often collaborated with architects and glassmakers, as at the 1925 Paris Exposition, where his several successful exhibits gained him worldwide recognition. His designs – executed in copper, bronze, gold and silver – often combined animal and human forms with floral and/or geometric patterns. Many of his surfaces were hammered in a decorative manner, as that of a lovely bronze platter which featured seaweed and other marine motifs. Brandt's most popular designs by far featured attractive human and animal forms, usually in openwork floral or foliated surrounds. He also made small andirons in the shape of cobras and jardinières with cobra handles. (The snake, taken from Egyptian art, was a popular Art Deco subject, also used by Jean Dunand, René Lalique, François-Emile Décorchement and others.)

BRANDT'S COLLABORATIONS

Through his father's involvement in an engineering firm, Brandt had early on developed an interest in working with metal. Most of his early work came from direct commissions by architects who needed metal fixtures for private houses and hotels. Brandt never lost his willingness to work with others, and, indeed, his best work was almost always the result of direct collaboration.

Many of his commissions demanded a highly developed sense of detail and the ability to work to a very strict set of limitations. At the same time as he was creating pairs of

Left: a detail from Edgar Brandt's L'Oasis *five-panel screen.*

Below: the La Tentation *floor lamp, designed by Brandt and Daum frères.*

Right: Classical volutes *figure on this hammered wrought-iron urn by Edgar Brandt.*

monumental doors, or wrought-iron staircases for the liners *Paris, Ile de France* and *Normandie*, Brandt would be designing more mundane pieces: grilles for indoor heating, radiator covers and other everyday objects. Some of his finest work was with the glass expert Antoine Daum. His cobra standard lamp, the coiling serpent acting as a foot, stem and holder for its Daum glass shade, is among one of his most striking creations.

Brandt had a deep respect for the aesthetic and moral heritage of French art, and saw it as his duty to keep France in the forefront of contemporary decorative design. He felt that industrial processes could be well used to serve this end, and sought constantly to ally art with industry. Many artists feared that the intro-duction of industrial techniques would lead

to mass-production which, they felt, would debase their art, but Brandt found this fear groundless. It was his conviction that artists could only benefit from an understanding of the mysteries and difficulties of production and also of the techniques of the machines.

THE 1925 EXPOSITION

He had himself served a long apprenticeship, not only in wrought-iron working, but also in silversmithing and jewellery-making, for which he had won prizes at the salons of the Société des Artistes Français. A man of phe-nomenal drive and energy, he executed both his own designs and those of others.

Although already well known before 1925, it was Brandt's varied and extensive work shown at the 1925 Exhibition that catapulted

him to the forefront of his field. He was com-missioned, with Ventre and Favier, to design the Porte d'Honneur (the gate of honour) for the Exposition, which they designed in col-laboration with René Lalique and Henri Navarre. The Porte d'Honneur was made of a 'staff', an inexpensive alloy, for the cost of iron in a project of this size and imperma-nence was prohibitive. Part of the challenge was to make the 'staff' look as fine as the ma-terial which it imitated. It was a great success, as were the other commissions that he carried out for the Exhibition. In particular, he was responsible for the acclaimed metal furniture and furnishings for the Ruhlmann pavilion. Another vital exhibit was his own pavilion, for which he designed an *ensemble* that included the spectacular and monumental five-panel screen *L'Oasis*, a highly refined fantasy of stylised flowers, foliage and fountains executed in brass and iron.

FERROBRANDT INC

The Brandt *ensemble* led to his first major commission in the United States, for what is known as either the Madison-Belmont or the Cheney Building, on the corner of Madison Avenue and 34th Street in Manhattan, where the exterior metalwork is still *in situ*. Cheney Brothers, a fabric house that occupied several floors in the building, also invited him to design their showrooms. This gave him the impetus to open Ferrobrandt Inc in New York. He expanded his operations in Paris at the same time, taking full advantage of all the publicity that evolved from his work at the Exposition.

BRANDT'S TECHNIQUE

His work was successful because Brandt understood the delicate balance between the monumental and the decorative. His extraordinary talent for balancing these two elements added great style to modern decoration. He was sometimes criticised for his use of industrial techniques, but his work was always redeemed by the beauty of the material, his meticulous attention to detail, and especially by the fine finished appearance of his pieces. This finish was achieved by an industrial technique that he perfected – oxyacetylene welding, which is all but invisible. In joining decorative elements, Brandt used hidden screws and bolts so that the eye was never distracted by details of construction.

Brandt exploited the tensile strengths of the material he used when designing furniture. Console tables, instead of standing solidly on four squat legs, could be treated more as open sculptures. Legs would be opened out with delicate filigree mouldings of fans and thistles filling the gaps, yet would still have enough strength to support the heavy weight of a thick slab of marble. Fire screens and doors could be reinterpreted to look almost like drawings suspended in air. Curling lines and leaves in door fronts seemed exquisitely delicate but had a strength and solidity fit for their purpose. Brandt also collaborated with Henri Favier on a series of decorative screens for which he provided the framework.

A COHESIVE STYLE

Another reason for the great success of Brandt's

Above: a wrought-iron table with a massive top of grey granite that is attributed to Raymond Subes.

Left: Raymond Subes designed this suite in bronze, wrought iron, marble and corduroy.

Above: an elaborately decorated hall stand, pedestal and wall sconces crafted in wrought iron by the naturalised French designer Paul Kiss in around 1925.

designs was his understanding of the relationship of each individual piece, such as a grille, staircase or chandelier, within an *ensemble* to the whole. Further objects designed by Brandt – including trays, paperknives, pendants, brooches, as well as other small items of jewellery – are testimony to the same inventiveness and sureness of hand that characterise his more monumental works.

RAYMOND SUBES

Raymond Subes was second only to Brandt in the scope and quality of his work. In 1919, at a relatively young age, he was appointed successor to Emile Robert as the director of the firm of Borderel et Robert.

Subes endeavoured to create an impression of richness and elegance in his work, but with great simplicity of technique. This aim was completely in accord with the economic and social conditions of the time, for the public demanded the maximum effect for the lowest price. Subes' solution was similar to that arrived at by Brandt: the marriage of artistic design to industrial technique. He found through his research that industrial processes could be used with very satisfactory results both in furniture and in more massive architectural works. This philosophy journeyed a long way from that of his mentor, Emile Robert, who had stubbornly scorned the use of anything but hand-held tools.

Subes devoted a great deal of time to the technical problems of his trade: how to produce the finest work, restrict costs as far as possible, and yet maintain artistic integrity. He aimed much of his research particularly at the uses of sheet metal, which could be formed by machine into any desired shape. Subes was also ingenious at using flat iron pieces to create works in series. Using

Left: an exotic bronze chair concocted by Armand-Albert Rateau. Apart from its cushion, it is awash with marine motifs.

Below: a silvered-bronze medallion made by Foucault and applied to an amboyna-wood veneered cabinet by Ruhlmann.

Above: the door of the Gulf Building in Houston is influenced by Edgar Brandt.

machines, Subes was able to produce pieces as cheaply as by casting. At the same time he understood that unique pieces must still be produced by hand, and he himself often took up the hammer to create powerful bas-reliefs for a door. A new type of metalwork had been born which allowed for production in series, and also made possible works too monumental to be executed at the forge.

PAUL KISS

Paul Kiss was born in Romania, but after studying in Paris became a naturalised Frenchman. His work explored the lyrical and expressive qualities that he saw in wrought iron, but was quite different in character to that of Brandt, with whom he collaborated early in his career. He exhibited a comprehensive range of wrought-iron furniture and lighting at the salons of the Société des Artistes Décorateurs and the Société des Artistes Français.

NICS FRÈRES

Jules and Michel Nics were Hungarian-born brothers who worked in Paris under the name of Nics Frères, producing a complete range of decorative ironwork, from furniture to architectural decoration. Their work was characterised by a highly conspicuous *martelé* (hand-hammered) decorative finish and a rather excessive use of natural forms, even after these had gone out of fashion. They rejected as heresy die-stamping and file work, and affirmed themselves as masters of the hammer, proud of their ability to make any piece by hand in a technique comparable to that of the finest artisans of the past.

Although Brandt was clearly the leader of the more traditional metalworkers, men like Subes, Adnet, Kiss, Rateau and Szabo produced work of great beauty. The most eccentric of this group by far was Armand-Albert Rateau. He constructed a bronze chaise-longue for Jeanne Lanvin's boudoir that rested, almost comically, on the backs of four deer. A washstand and mirror piece was modelled from two peacocks standing back to back, their two heads holding the mirror.

With metal, anything was possible, but the bizarre examples of Rateau were way out of keeping with the clean and practical furniture of Le Corbusier or Eileen Gray. Elegance was not just the domain of the intricate foliage of a Brandt screen, a Kiss cabinet or a Subes mantelpiece clock: it could be seen to even greater effect in an oak table top supported by just two sheets of bent metal by Louis Sognot. It was minimal, reduced to the contrast between the two materials used: the shiny, cold metal and the rich patina and grain of the wood.

There were also various Art Deco medallists working in silver, bronze and other materials, not only in France but also in Britain, Germany and the United States. The Hungarian-born Tony Szirmai, who was based in Paris, specialised in commemorative pieces;

Pierre Turin produced silver, copper and bronzed-metal plaques, often octagonal, which featured stylised figures and flowers; while André Lavrillier created a handsome medal depicting Leda and the swan.

BAUHAUS METALWORKERS

At the Bauhaus, Wilhelm Wagenfeld, an architect and industrial designer, was especially associated with the metal workshop from 1922 to about 1931, when he left to work with glass and ceramics. He fashioned a hammered-copper coffee machine in 1923 which is so futuristic in appearance that it could be a prototype for an astronaut's helmet.

Marianne Brandt of the Bauhaus is, however, perhaps the best-known German metalworker. Surprisingly, she turned her supreme design skills to rather mundane objects, such as ashtrays, shaving mirrors and cooking utensils. The most famous is her *Kandem* bedside lamp, which, with its push-button switch and adjustable reflector/shade, is the forerunner of so many similar lamps today.

Above: a wrought-iron candelabrum made by William Hunt Diederich during the 1920s. His work was characterised by its sharp, silhouetted imagery.

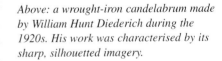

Left: a Zephyr digital clock designed by Kem Weber for Lawson, Time, Inc, c.1933.

Above: Monel metal sheathes a lift interior at Unilever House, London. The panels on the right depict modern transportation.

Right: a four-tubed bud vase, which was mass-produced in various metals by Chase Brass & Copper Co of Connecticut.

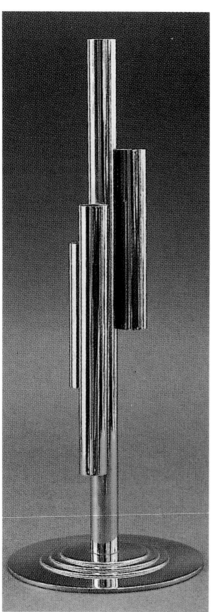

AMERICAN METALWORK

Although the United States lagged behind France in its adoption of metalwork for interiors, the influence of the 1925 Paris Exposition and the opening of Edgar Brandt's New York office stimulated a taste for this highly versatile area of the decorative arts. By the late 1920s, it had become immensely popular, and there were a number of American designers and craftsmen who were producing a great variety of both interior and exterior ironwork.

Large-scale metalwork in America – gates, architectural elements and such – were much influenced by the Parisian designs of Brandt, Subes and other *ferronniers*. Their impact can be clearly discerned on the designers at the Rose Iron Works in Cleveland, Ohio, whose screens and tables are blatant imitations of Brandt's works.

OSCAR BACH

Oscar Bach was perhaps the only craftsman in this field who could match the technical mastery of the great French ironworkers. Born in Germany, he enjoyed a successful career there before coming to the United States in 1914. He opened a studio in New York, where he was soon flooded with private and commercial commissions. Proficient in many metals and styles of metalwork, he used copper, aluminium, bronze, chrome and nickel silver to provide colour and textural contrast in the decorative elements he designed. His contribution to many of New York's most outstanding buildings is immeasurable.

Other noted American metalworkers included William Hunt Diederich and Kem Weber. William Hunt Diederich emigrated to the United States from Hungary when he was 15 and took up residence in Boston with his grandfather, William Morris Hunt, who was

an artist. Diederich was a successful designer in many areas, but was particularly attracted
to metalwork. His simple, two-dimensional
figures and animals seem snipped out of iron.
With their sharp, jagged edges and minimal
surface decoration they have a lively vitality
that reflects their creator's personality and love
of animal subjects.

In contrast, Weber's designs for clocks (including digital ones in the 1930s), lamps, tea
and coffee sets, as well as furniture. were sleekly functional. Even the smallest of items, such
as a stepped clock case of brass and chromed
metal, was impeccably designed and
undeniably 'machine age'.

COMMERCIAL METALWORK

Further Modernist influences can be seen in
the designs of the Chase Brass & Copper
Company in Waterbury, Connecticut, which
employed famous as well as obscure designers. It produced a wide range of useful wares
known for their 'beautility' – cigarette boxes,
ashtrays, cocktail shakers, wine coolers,
kitchen utensils, candlesticks and vases. Its
designs were wonderfully *moderne*, architectonic, Cubist and crisp. A bud vase of 1936,
for example, consists of four chrome pipes
that are attached to each other at uneven
angles and rest on a circular base.

Many American metalworkers were
engaged in gigantic architectural projects for
which they often turned to materials other than
the traditional iron, bronze, brass and copper.
Aluminium, chromium, cadmium and 'monel'
metal (a nickel-copper alloy), among others,

*Right: a radiator grille designed by Jacques
Delamarre for New York's Chanin Building,
1929, that reproduces in brass the exterior
of the building.*

Above: a tiled executive bathroom in the Chanin Building in New York. Its decoration was supervised by Jacques Delamarre and the geometric motifs that adorn it echo the details of the building's metalwork features (see page 61).

all came into play, sometimes used as thin sheetings (or plates) over another metal. Numerous components of New York skyscrapers – elevators, mail boxes, doors and so on – were made of these new metals, used either on their own or in combination with other materials. Some of these (often anonymous) creations, with their geometric, floral and figural grillework, have come to be considered among the most outstanding examples of Art Deco in the United States, and can be seen in New York's Chanin and Daily News buildings, as well as in countless other structures throughout the country.

DINANDERIE

Yet it was not only new, non-precious metals with which designers worked – a number of whom were proficient in *dinanderie* (named after the Flemish town of Dinant). Many of the techniques of metal encrustation were of ancient origin, and by returning to old traditions and reinterpreting them differently, twentieth-century artists were able to produce works of a singular vitality.

The interest in Japanese art that began during the late nineteenth century had much to do with the resurgence of interest in *dinanderie*, as well as in lacquer. Jean Dunand, who was to become the most important artist to work in both these techniques, was introduced to the medium by the Japanese lacquerer Sougawara. He quickly mastered the technique of lacquering and his fascination with this and *dinanderie* produced some of the most extraordinary objects of his, or any other, time. Obviously the lacquer had to be applied to a surface, and Dunand began with vases, all made by hand in the *dinanderie* technique. His earliest vases derived their shape from gourds and other vegetal forms, and he often worked the surfaces with repoussé, chiselling, patinas of browns and greens and inlays of other metals either to highlight the naturalistic form or to produce such organically inspired motifs as scales and peacock feathers. His forms gradually became simpler and his designs more geometric, relying on surface ornamentation and applied metal for effect.

GOULDEN, FAURÉ AND LINOSSIER
Jean Goulden created clocks, lamps, boxes and other *objets* in metal, often embellished with coloured enamelling, a process he learned from Dunand, with whom he sometimes collaborated. His avant-garde, highly angular works often resembled Cubist and Constructivist sculpture. Camille Fauré also worked with enamel on metal, but, unlike Goulden's pieces, his vessels were dominated by the coloured enamel.

Claudius Linossier was a master of the art of *dinanderie*, who had been an apprentice metalworker in his native Lyons when only 13 years old, and had mastered embossing, engraving, enamelling, metal encrustation, repoussé and all the other metalwork techniques. The most outstanding element of his work is his use of metal encrustation. He loved the subtle play of one tone against another, and as silver and copper provided only a limited palette, he began to develop his own alloys, using ingots he cast himself, and fashioning thin plaquettes that he graded by tone.

SERRIÈRE AND MERGIER
Another silversmith who occasionally worked in base metals, often with silver inlays, was Jean Serrière. His objects, mainly trays and bowls, are massive in feeling and of extremely simple design, enlivened by traces of the hand work that formed them. Paul-Louis Mergier,

Above: A lampshade with a beaten-metal dinanderie *base made by the versatile designer Jean Dunand.*

Left: A yellow-metal powder compact and cigarette case made by the Elgin American firm in Illinois.

an aeronautical engineer who painted, designed and made furniture, also found time for *dinanderie* work. His vases are simple in form, and his preferred subjects were stylised figures and animals defined by various patinas, inlaid silver and lacquer, often executed by the well-known Japanese artist Hamanaka.

DAURAT'S PEWTER

Maurice Daurat was an artist who chose to work in pewter. Pewter is a soft metal, ductile and extremely supple, and Daurat exploited its almost flesh-like surface and its potential for sombre shadows and irregular reflections of light from hammer marks, finding that these imparted a warmth more appealing than the cold gleam of silver. His designs became increasingly refined until they were almost a series of exercises in form and simplicity. His minimal concessions to ornament were a ring of beads at the base, or an interestingly designed handle. He intended his pieces to be admired rather than used, and in his hand pewter indeed achieved the status of a new-found material and could stand next to the finest silver without shame.

Above: A jewel-like, enamel-on-copper vase by Camille Fauré.

Right: A silver and jade soup tureen created by Jean Puiforcat.